Senatorial Character:

A SERMON

IN

West Church, Boston,

Sunday, 15th of March,

AFTER THE

DECEASE OF CHARLES SUMNER.

By C. A. BARTOL.

BOSTON:
A. WILLIAMS & CO., 135 WASHINGTON STREET.
1874.

SERMON.

"*He made him to teach his senators wisdom.*" — PSALMS CV, 21, 22.

THE common theory of the pulpit is of a place devoted to expound some old situation, abstract scheme of salvation, or article in a creed. It has a higher end, — to give the meaning of the scenes of real life, in which we observe the actors and play ourselves a part. If history be philosophy teaching by example, and of all history biography be the soul, then human character, when rare and conspicuous in its traits or achievements, gives as pattern or warning the chief lesson. Christian edification comes less signally from hair-splitting, dogmatic distinction than from contemplating for imitation or admonition the lives of Enoch and Solomon, Paul and Peter, Jesus and John. So I take to-day the death of the most eminent civilian of Massachusetts for my theme.

As the King in Egypt chose Joseph to teach his senators wisdom, no man of late years has equalled Charles Sumner as an instructor or influence in the Senate of the United States.

An instinct of nature prompts us to make some account and sum up the significance of any one's career, privately, on the domestic stage, or before the people, if he has challenged attention in a larger sphere.

It may be useful to make some discriminating estimate of Mr. Sumner's contributions to the public good, the legislature of a free State in a great Union being the monarch that for so long a period continued to elect him to his high office.

However opinions may differ of his prudence or ability, the weight of his word or importance of his position none will doubt.

Our messenger of the lightning had no greater task this last week in the world than to wait at his threshold and run with news every hour over the wires of his estate.

His principal peers at his bedside and his colored clients flocking for inquiry at his door showed a feeling of love and sympathy reaching from the highest to the lowest class.

In culture he was a match for nobles, in temper he was a champion of the oppressed and friend to the poor.

I suppose no American name is more widely known and celebrated in all civilized lands.

Great Britain and France will feel the shock of his decease.

That one of our political pillars has fallen will be

known at the Court of St. Petersburg and among the counsellors of Berlin.

Italy and Spain, with their Republican struggles and aims, will miss an advocate on this side the sea.

Castelar will mourn the departure of a companion in arms in the peaceful battles of reform, as Cavour might have felt through the cable from him for emancipation an electric touch.

South America, with her strange mixture of barbarism with liberation, will be conscious of owing some honor to the obsequies of a sympathizer with all that is generous in her aspirations.

Hayti will deplore the decease of a supporter of her rights more powerful than any on her own shores.

A flutter of pain and sorrow will pass through that whole flock of islands alighted, as in the great harbor of our land, betwixt the Gulf of Mexico and the Caribbean Sea.

So it will be because not only a man, a citizen of the Commonwealth and foremost trustee in the Congress of the country, but a cosmopolite is dead, deserving that name as truly as any man who, since the settlement of these colonies, has lived within their bounds.

What is the reason of the wide consequence of this event?

Not in the man's extraordinary original power.

Nature did not intend aught intellectually pre-eminent in his constitution.

It had no organic strength to strike out new paths in action or expression.

It fell into ways other agents had broken.

Mr. Sumner was not even an aboriginal abolitionist; he joined and did yeoman's service in the antislavery ranks.

He startled the soldiers, twenty-nine years ago, in Boston, with his extreme doctrine of peace; but he followed Ladd and others, with copious illustration, but no new sentiment or novel idea.

Of origination there is no speck in his reflections or spark in his style.

His mind is parasitical, his discourse full of precedents, quotations, classic scenes, and historic allusions, sometimes savoring of schoolboy recitations, sophomoric and declamatory, stilted and grotesque. Yet he is in the list of wonderful men. Others thought and he was led to fancy some resemblance in his feature and person to Edmund Burke, which the portrait of Mr. Burke might actually suggest; but this resemblance to the great English Commoner was but skin-deep, with little hint of the deep sea line that fathomed every question, or the impassioned imagination which cast the light of flame on every measure, and kindled with magnetic sympathy, against the French Revolution and for American privilege, now one and now another portion of the British realm.

Mr. Sumner was perhaps a greater lover of freedom in its principle as an inherent right and claim of all mankind than Mr. Burke; but Burke had pre-eminent genius in politics, Sumner only accomplished talent, though in the later light of a more humane era put to service in a grander cause.

Shakespeare, Milton, Bacon, Newton, Burke, Wiiliam Blake: such would be our shining classification for poetry, philosophy, science, politics, art, in the mother land.

But for native force we should think of many persons before Sumner in his own field of study and pursuit.

He had not the majestic sweep of Webster, the weight or heat of that mountain with its base of granite and flame, the fiery eloquence of Clay, the close grip of John Quincy Adams in argument, or the subtile felicity and gleam of primary perception which William Henry Seward brought for the enlivening of debate.

He never could have invented the New-Yorker's phrase of *The Irrepressible Conflict* as applied to the Free and Slave States, or the Illinoisian Abraham Lincoln's grander adaptation of Scripture,—*A house divided against itself cannot stand: I do not expect the house to fall, but to cease to be divided.*

Mr. Sumner quoted abundantly, but he is not for any rhetorical merits or ideal inventions in the whole range of his voluminous works quotable, however rich in his right to be cited for the spirit and design on every page.

He stands not strong among men of strength, thinkers and benefactors at first hand, germinators of thought and heroism in the van of the race,— such as bear the stamp of a primitive and primeval energy, like Abraham, Noah, Moses, David and Paul, Buddha and Mohammed, Socrates and Plato, in the East; Garrison and John Brown among ourselves.

He was an orator of the conceptions of his predecessors and superiors, an arguer of the case, a sheriff to execute a writ.

One name I do not mention in this comparison, because, being neither ancient nor modern, it is greatest of all.

But if his were a secondary mind, a vine round a stouter trunk, how like some such creeper it towered and grew, appropriated nourishment and vigor from the old decaying boughs, till at length, with superior toughness and tenacity, it could breast every breeze, and stood proudly alone!

Yet his understanding was that not of the revealer, but the scholar to the last. He imparted what he learned; he knew what he had been told. His delivery was not, like Patrick Henry's, a bolt from Heaven to rend the obstacle and burn up opposition, but a crystal stream flowing smoothly from some rock that had garnered up the mountain-dew and the rain; and he completely informed if he did not like Fisher Ames irresistibly charm.

But in the moral region lay the real greatness of the man. His conscience was original and he had no original sin.

No imputation on his purpose but cleared away like the cloud from a breath on spotless steel, leaving the metal bright as before.

He was as incorruptible as he honorably said to me was Fessenden, his great rival in the Senate; and when he also one day, speaking of his limited means, remarked: "I have never had the art to get my hands into the Treasury," I was fain to answer, "You the whole man are in the Treasury yourself." He was indeed in our politics a fund and never-broken bank of moral wealth. Justice was his inspiration. He was a prophet by equity. Righteousness was his genius; and humanity, in any lack of imagination, his insight and foresight. He was without spot. He wore ermine though he sat not on the bench. John Jay had not cleaner hands, nor John Marshall a more honest will; Hamilton and Jefferson were no more patriotic in contending than he in every legal or congressional strife; and Story, his favorite teacher, and whose favorite pupil he was, no more opulent in knowledge or innocent in its use.

As an antagonist, handling questions of motive or policy, he was as frank as the lion-hearted Richard and simple as a child.

From those early debates to which I listened, on prison discipline, thirty years ago, to his latest speech on the Centennial Exhibition, this candor, amounting to generosity and magnanimity, was plain as the sun.

He had no tricks, no management, no intrigue. He showed his hand.

Could he not prevail by openness and sincerity, he would not prevail at all.

If he started no new ideas or measures that have been adopted precisely in the way he conceived, or shape he gave, he mightily sustained all good ones, and of their goodness he would not abate a tithe.

Of this rectitude benignity was the crown. Sternly exposing what he thought mean or unworthy in any proceeding or adversary, his severity was in his argument and rhetoric rather than in the feeling of his soul.

Without a sweet disposition no man could have had such a smile. Without some grandeur of design no man ever displayed such a countenance and port, handsome and sublime. In his intentness and earnestness, he did not suspect the liability of his expressions to the charge of a vindictiveness he was unconscious of in his own breast. It was like a philippic of Demosthenes; it was a Ciceronian oration against some Catiline, real or supposed. A poetic sort of revenge was all he meant to take, although his language to opponents, whom perhaps he sometimes mistook, may be subject to blame. Pity he was so devoid of humor to recommend or soften his strokes!

His old peace doctrine, doubtless, mainly prompted his battle-flag resolution, while the time of offering it and his nearly contemporaneous break with his party seemed to betray an unfair and personal bias of which he was unaware.

Sensible of his great and long importance to the government, an egoistic, assuming, imperious, irascible inclination may to some have appeared to be disclosed; but he ingenuously felt he had a title to be consulted and that it was a slight and insult to set him aside. Let the administration that refused him as an instrument beware lest it become a hammer in the hands of inferior men, whose success will be suicide, and itself the tool! This may an inspiration from his coffin prevent! Massachusetts has honored herself at least as much as she did her son, and cast from yonder halls one ray of comfort on his seat in the Senate and on his death-bed in rescinding the censure on his course; for his memory is among her trophies, — no banner more so that hangs beneath the cupola above the marble floor,— and she is the inheritor of his renown; for if "Providence made Washington childless that the country might call him father," Sumner is without offspring that the State may be his mourner.

This freedom from all selfish heat or hate, one distinction of the statesman from the politician, is a trait too rare to pass without emphasis and applause.

An example, indeed, to the ordinary run of village contrivers, caucus packers, and municipal aspirants, of a man who never pulled a wire, rolled a log, laid a pipe, listened in a lobby, whispered in the ear what might not be proclaimed on the house-top, held a man by the button, or blew any trumpet but of the public good, however in his magnificent self-respect he might be falsely accused of wishing to blow only his own!

If a jealous personal honor ever had apology or excuse, it was how ample and entire in the case of a man— the only one in our annals — appointed to wear the shining crown of martyrdom before his translation, to get up out of his own blood and recover from the foul assassin's bludgeon after medical tortures of the surgeon's moxa in combustion on his disabled spine, such as Sequard says he never applied to any other living creature.*

So he rose to bear the same unflinching testimony, no more groaning under the fire of reproach than of the burning cotton; and if proud of his position, with perfect consistency modest too.

I did not and at this distance of cooling time do not approve all the phraseology he employed on that senatorial occasion; but his weapons were words, and, however rough and affronting, for the right: those of his foes, equally gross and injurious, were for the wrong; and the assault of brutal force came to disturb the equation, in violation of all parliamentary privilege, with Douglas and his piratical compeers, with ill-disguised pleasure and half-pretended unconcern, looking on their own ignominy, crime, and shame, while the martyr that all but, yet not quite, expired, after years of suffering comes back, a resurrection witness not disposed of, and the assailant and would-be executioner dies long first, in Northern and Southern disgrace and his own remorse.

---

* "Will chloroform make the operation less beneficial?" he asked. "I could not lie," said the Doctor, 'and said, Yes."—"Then I will not take it," he replied.

At the same height with Milton in his blindness, Sumner, with his torn and aching nerves, like a soldier who will not leave the field for loss of blood, resumed the conflict, struggling with disappointment and sorrow in age and loneliness, still moving ever immediately against all the powers of evil and works of the devil, his white plume, like that of the French Prince he quoted, floating ever ahead to follow; like ex-President, Representative Adams, in his armor to the very edge and last of earth, like Buckle, talking in his agony of his book, and commending to survivors in Congress his beloved Civil Rights' Bill, dealing out well-directed blows for his race of every color and tribe till the instant the final stroke came to cut body and spirit apart. Truly, the halo of angelic glory hangs not only around the heads of dead saints! Such a man might be tempted to claim the honor of his fellow-men, and a lofty self-esteem and aspiration to the highest dignities hardly misbecame him, who, like Cato, was wrapped in conscious integrity, and established in the respect of all praiseworthy persons such a place. After the famous eulogy in his Phi Beta Kappa oration, of Pickering, Story, Allston, and Channing, the toast of John Quincy Adams was: "The memory of the scholar, jurist, artist, and divine, — and not the memory, but the long life of the kindred genius that has embalmed them all." Yet it has come for him also to a memory, and a noble one now.

As a humble cotemporary I copy not others' impressions, but simply set down my own. Among his associates, the fault commonly found with Sumner is not that he was implacable—none easier to propitiate—but impracticable; not an idealist, but ideologist and doctrinary dreamer of a peace and freedom on earth which he put into no effective and satisfactory form; for ten thousand besides him recommended the Emancipation, which John Quincy Adams held justifiable as a war measure, and Lincoln proclaimed.

But though the greatness of rulers and social founders is in what they establish and bring to pass, yet in default of this rare achievement, which happens seldom in the course of ages to any man, a certain impracticability is in others in many exigencies a blessing to be thankful for, a virtue to applaud. In the collisions of interest with principle are plenty to trim, compromise, and compound as oligarchs or demagogues bid; but as the merit of some substances is the lack of ductility, so how oft we must lean on unmalleable men, whose back-bone is not supple as a universal joint, who will not "crook the pregnant hinges of the knee where thrift may follow fawning," and who, in a noble discontent with all yet undertaken or done, summon to worthier performance towards never-attained perfection in betterment of the common lot. Mr. Rubinstein was displeased with the preacher who said, "Men must be expected to do no more than they can." "No," said the artist, "that doctrine letting down the standard is worse than actual vice. We can forgive the last, not the first!" Men must do the *impossible*, — a word which Napoleon told his officer was beastly, never to be spoken, and in his dictionary not found. "With God all things are possible," and that means possible to whoever works with Him. Said the pianist to his pupils, "If you do not expect or intend to write finer music than Beethoven, you have no business to compose at all." Mr. Sumner aimed at the sun; and the feeling of philanthropic duty with which he stirred the body politic out of the custom of chronic oppression and old habit of wrong was of more precious consequence than carrying any particular scheme. With this earnestness, that would not stop short of improving the world, I was struck in my last conversation with him on the threatened Spanish war. If he did not interest or magnetize everybody, all individuals, like Crittenden or Clay, few cared more for their kind; and this broad benevolence, as well as special affection, lays hold on immortality. Who shall say such as Agassiz and Sumner are dead? "A great man has fallen," said my friend: no, a good man has risen.

Death brings simplicity and reality. As it approaches, learning and philosophy go; goodness and conscience are left, the last guests in the feast of life at the table of the heart. In Sumner the *sentiment*, foremost always, blooms at the pillow where last he laid, "so tired and weary," his head; and sentiment, as well as science, has eternal claim. He extends courtesy to callers, opens his eye while it could open, waves his hand while it had strength to move, says *Sit down* to his old associate, tries to speak when the lips no longer obey the will, and sends a legacy of love and reverence more precious than any gold to his old friend. *Cold* was he indeed?

For his noble affections, how we shall remember the solitary and little-related man, with no children, when he was sad, to play with in his house! His thirst for knowledge, his bent to investigate and study whatever had been said and done in the world, would have made him an antiquarian save for his patriotic and humanitarian zeal.

What a lover and knower he was of pictures, bronzes, manuscripts, old books, curious relics of the past, all memorials in all time of his fellow-men! Such research is a sort of humanity. Yet no man's sympathies were more in the present than his, or more eager to stretch after a perfected civilization in the future.

Indeed, the millennial day shone so upon him through the vista of hope as to dazzle and blind him, like Saul on the road to Damascus, to the immediate possibilities of action and direct bearings of his theme.

If there were any defect in his style, it was a certain lack of proportion, or an exceeding uniform stress, a straining forward against the leash of irrefragable circumstance, till in the ardor of pursuit the perspective of the subject was lost.

But whatever might be the lesser vices, the great virtues were in his judgment and thought.

He was an admirable inciter. How we needed incentives! He hallooed to a grander chase than any huntsman's. He was the Lamartine of America, *our* orator of the human race. The Senate floor was to him a popular rostrum and sacred stump. He advocated every great cause if he found the key of none.

He roused England and the United States, kindling into white heat, like dry wood, after such long seasoning, the Alabama difficulties, and compelling an attention which doubtless was good for both parties, although his extravagant statement of the doctrine of consequential damages could not settle the question, and failed of the seal and sanction of international law.

More human than divine, his inspiration came from without rather than from within. The first time I saw him, forty years ago, with the same characteristic ornate and fervent language, and garnish of Latin references, he elucidated to me the difference between a pettifogger or litigious searcher for cases — a *præco actionum* as he called him — and a jurist of the Judge Story stamp.

Already he saw in faith the career for which he turned aside from every flattering offer that would divert him, conscious of superior ability to serve at the highest posts to which Democrat joined hands with Free Soiler to lead. Strange that the seemingly accidental, shall I say insincere, vote of a coalition should have furnished the most distinguished and perhaps longest continued Senator of the land!

His empty chair on the Senate floor, drew, last week, at the obsequies, the spectators' eyes.

But it was unoccupied that he might fill a higher seat prepared, waiting for, and needing, not the undying part but the everlasting whole; for we are not *whole* till we drop our dust! Three funeral-sensations, I remember,— of Webster, the man of power, Lincoln, the man of providence, and Sumner, as I delight to call him, the man of purity.

If the shadow of no demise ever brooded over this

region as a huge pall, a black sheet let down from the sky, like that of the great New-Englander; and if no public sorrow in our day and generation was ever keener than when the martyr-president gave up the ghost at the revengeful stroke of the monster of political slavery, expiring, like a leviathan, under his hand; never was a more genuine tribute than will be laid on the Senator's tomb, or a completer satisfaction in an ended testimony and finished work, whatever part he left for us to finish. Several years ago, forced by illness away from the theatre of public duties and affairs into a country refuge, as the sounds came softened by distance from the arena at the capitol where the combatants struggled together, however pleasantly fell the counsels of moderation and prudence on my ear, I recognized the clarion of Sumner, urging to absolute truth and honor, and, far or near, resounding above them all.

Here was a man that could not bend or yield, alloy or qualify, surrender or retreat. Here was an incorruptibility proof against bribes, and too original in legislatives halls, an originality, if not of suggestion yet of heroic act. Here was an obstinacy not of will, but idea; for ideas are more obstinate than any human will in the world. Here was a necessity not of whim but duty, such as was laid on the great apostle to the Gentiles to preach the Gospel, and drove Luther to the Diet of Worms. I aim at simple truth as I speak. Such stubbornness will surely accomplish great results and always fetch an echo from the human breast. I abstain from overstatement. Love must not falsify or exaggerate. It is no compliment to exalt another by belying ourselves. Our friend belongs to history now; and the offerings of a discriminating respect are part of its material. I must think of him less as hewn by the Divinity than carving himself. Like one of the straws a swallow bears to build its nest, let my poor word go to the fashioning by many hands, of the niche of his fame. His head had its limits; but there was no outside to his heart! The great man's servant, secretary, keeper of his house, farmer of his estate, has something valuable to say of him; and the humblest coeval's contribution will not be refused or despised. Voicing the feeling of no party, for him or against, I but touch the ground of that secret respect to his character and aim which not only favorers but foes are constrained, unitedly, unanimously, instinctively, to pay.

> "Little heeds he what is said;
> They have done with all below;"

Such were the commonplaces of the old theology

founded on the notion of a senseless rest of the dead, or their departure to an infinite distance from our earthly abode. But we reconsider such views. He, who was so sensitive to his fellow-citizens' regard, can hardly be insensible now, or unconscious of our sincere honor. I would speak as in his presence and to his ear! His clear voice will be no longer heard in our assemblies, or his commanding form cast its welcome shadow through our streets.

But the moral stature, with which, as in mental height, he transcended the common sons of men, shall be seen and felt.

Nor can the recollection for ages pass how, as a brave knight, with superb courage, horsed on ideas for the saving of the land, he flung defiance from boldness unsurpassed at the giant wrong, — that dragon and old serpent, the form Satan took for us, the *Barbarism of Slavery*, and *Slavery sectional not national*, as he entitled the greatest speeches he made. His somewhat artificial manner, method, and phrase only clothed or cloaked an indigenous force of conscience, which was a piece of nature, a divine monolith or monogram, if his intellect were not. His meaning no man, white or black, in the land doubted or could misunderstand.

If his forensic efforts had been to a nice taste better in some respects, the improvement might have made them in others for general effect worse or of less effect. They were at least faithfully prepared from a width of observation and stock of information seldom equalled, and set forth with a consecutive order of formal logic worthy of a master in the schools.

Twice has been his conspicuous entry into this town: first, after he was outraged for his freedom of utterance in his place; next, yesterday, in whatever connection the spirit may have with the forsaken robe which it cannot desert or lose all feeling for at once.

How, but as a man of principle, shall he stand forever in our memory and in the human mind? Let his name, like that of Washington, be a lasting rebuke to venality, selfish ambition, bribery, and all political intrigue! He is one more added to the band of blessed bigots which, wiser than any conformists, all our pilgrim fathers were.

"You can rest soon," he said to the familiar friend and companion in clerkly labor who was rubbing the hands fast growing cold in death. No chafing can restore what turns to the clay of which it was made. The flowers you form into his name will fade, but to cherish his honor we will never cease. Let his body be "buried in peace: his name liveth evermore."

www.ingramcontent.com/pod-product-compliance
Lightning Source LLC
LaVergne TN
LVHW011147110826
845150LV00008B/2552

9781418191900